Michael Jordan
The Best Ever

by Sarah Houghton

Reading Consultant:
Timothy Rasinski, Ph.D.
Professor of Reading Education
Kent State University

Capstone Curriculum Publishing

Capstone Curriculum Publishing materials are published by Capstone Press, P.O. Box 669, 151 Good Counsel Drive, Mankato, Minnesota, 56002
http://www.capstone-press.com

Library of Congress Cataloging-in-Publication Data
Houghton, Sarah, 1978-
    Michael Jordan: the best ever/by Sarah Houghton
    p. cm.
    Includes bibliographical references (p. 62) and index.
    Summary: Tells the story of basketball superstar Michael Jordan, from his youth to his highly successful professional career, which includes six NBA titles and numerous records and awards.
    ISBN 0-7368-9502-7 (pbk.)—ISBN 0-7368-4002-8 (hardcover)
    1. Jordan, Michael, 1963—Juvenile literature. 2. Basketball players—United States—Biography—Juvenile literature. [1. Jordan, Michael, 1963- 2. Basketball players. 3. African Americans—Biography.] I. Title.
GV884.J67 H68 2002
796.323'092—dc21
                                                                2001002929

Created by Kent Publishing Services, Inc.
Designed by Signature Design Group, Inc.

This publisher has made every effort to trace ownership of all copyrighted material and to secure necessary permissions. In the event of any questions arising as to the use of any material, the publisher, while expressing regret for any inadvertent error, will be happy to make necessary corrections.

Photo Credits:
Cover, Jed Jacobcohn/Allsport; page 4, AFP/Corbis; pages 10-11, 13, 14, Photo Copyright—Wilmington Star-News/Used by permission; pages 16, 23, Wally McNamee/Corbis; pages 18, 24, 26, 58-59, Corbis/Bettmann; page 30, Fred Jewell/AP Laserphoto; pages 32, 36, Jonathon Daniel/Allsport; page 39, S. Carmona/Corbis; page 42, Scott Wachter/Corbis; page 45, Todd Warshaw/ Allsport; page 46, Robert Sullivan/Corbis; page 51, Jeff Haynes/Corbis; page 55, John Zich/Corbis; page 57, Andrew Wallace/Reuters Photo Archive

Printed in the United States of America.

2 3 4 5 6 07 06 05 04 03 02

Table of Contents

— Chapter **1** —

Learning to Fly

Michael Jordan wanted to be the best basketball player in the world. He wanted to fly. Some people say that he can! But it took hard work and sacrifice. Here is the story of a man who became the best ever.

An Ordinary Boy

Michael Jeffrey Jordan was born on February 17, 1963. His parents, James and Deloris, lived in Brooklyn, New York. Soon after Michael's birth, the family moved to Wilmington, North Carolina.

Both James's and Deloris's parents had been sharecroppers. They knew all about hard work. James got a job with General Electric. Deloris worked in a bank. Both worked hard at their jobs, and they did well.

---

sharecropper: a person who farms land owned by another person

Growing Up

Michael had a happy childhood. He was close to his parents, two brothers, and two sisters. Michael loved sports, just like his dad did. His favorite sport was baseball.

Deloris made all her children help with the chores. She believed discipline would make her children stronger adults. At the time, there was no way she could know this discipline would later help Michael become a star athlete. There was no way anyone could know that Michael Jeffrey Jordan was going to fly.

---

discipline: control over the way a person behaves

The Rack

Michael's dad built a basketball court in the family's backyard. Michael and his brother Larry played for hours every day. They were proud of their court. They called it "the Rack."

Michael never, ever won. Larry was older and taller than Michael. He dribbled faster, jumped higher, and shot better. Larry gave Michael tips, but he never let his brother win. Michael knew he would have to get a lot better to beat his brother.

The First Dunk

The brothers simply loved to play basketball. Their parents knew this. They told Michael and Larry that in order to play, they had to get good grades, too.

Michael became extremely competitive. He desperately wanted to be good. Most of all he wanted to beat Larry.

As the months went by, the games got closer and closer. Larry still won, but that made Michael try harder. He enjoyed the challenge. Eventually, the work paid off. Michael started to beat Larry.

One day Michael dunked for the very first time on the backyard court, right over Larry's head. Soon Michael wanted to beat Larry's taller friends. He had to slowly build up his skills. But he liked to be tested. He would never quit. Michael started to win more often.

---

competitive: badly wanting to win; always seeking to do better than others
desperately: with a willingness to do anything

Rising above Racism

One day, Michael got into a fight with a girl from school. The girl had called him "nigger." Michael lost his temper and squashed a Popsicle® into the girl's hair. He was suspended from school.

Michael's parents explained that there was racism in the world. But he had to rise above it. He should be better than that.

Michael's parents told him that it doesn't matter what color someone is on the outside. It's what's inside that counts. They taught Michael to be color-blind when it came to race. He listened to their advice.

In Trouble Again

Michael's love for basketball grew stronger in high school. He even started cutting class to shoot baskets. He was suspended from school again. His parents took this very seriously.

Michael and his mother and father

Michael's parents knew he got into trouble because he was so competitive. He skipped classes because he wanted to be the best. But they helped him see that to be the best he would have to go to college. To do that, he would need good grades. College became another challenge. Michael started working harder at school. He began to do well in class and on the court.

Not Good Enough

Michael tried out for the varsity basketball team at Laney High School. He didn't make the team. Michael was surprised and angry. This made him want to succeed even more. Just like when he was playing his brother Larry, Michael worked harder because someone had beaten him.

Michael continued to work hard on both his grades and his game. He shot hoops every spare minute he had. He went to extra training sessions with coaches.

In the summer between 10th and 11th grades, Michael grew 4 inches (10 centimeters). In the fall, he tried out for the varsity team again. This time he made it. His hard work had paid off.

But once on the team, Michael did not play very well. Despite his hard work to make the team, he still needed to get better.

---

varsity: the main team that represents a school

Michael finally made the varsity team in high school, but he knew he had to get better.

Michael Jordan playing for Laney High School

The First "Shot"

One holiday tournament, Laney High School played its arch rival, New Hanover High. The game was very close. In the fourth quarter, Michael felt the intensity of the game. His competitive juices took over. He scored basket after basket. With just seconds left in the game, Laney only trailed by one point. Then, the ball went to Michael.

Michael looked up at the basket. The defenders swarmed around him. Calmly, he shot the ball. It swished through the net. The buzzer sounded. Laney had won, and Michael had made "the shot." This was his first game-winning shot. But it wouldn't be his last.

---

intensity: strong feelings
defender: a player who tries to keep the other team from scoring

Patrick Ewing of Georgetown guards Michael.

Chapter 2

College Star

Michael has said that he learned a lot in high school. But he also said that his parents taught him even more. What lessons have your parents taught you? If you were a parent, what lessons would you teach your children?

On to College

It was 1981 and time for Michael to go off to college. He decided to go to the University of North Carolina (UNC). Michael liked the campus at UNC. He also liked the basketball coach.

Several other colleges had offered Michael scholarships. Coaches even offered him a starting position to come to their school. However, Coach Dean Smith of UNC didn't offer Michael a starting spot on his team. Michael respected that. It made him want to work hard.

Playing Ill

It was rare for a freshman to make the team at UNC. But Michael made the team. He also made the starting line-up. He played well until the last two weeks of the season. Then he became ill.

An important game against the University of Georgia approached. Doctors wanted to put Michael in the hospital. Instead, he played. He scored 18 points, and the UNC Tar Heels won.

Michael Jordan won several awards as a college player. He was named Rookie of the Year in 1982. In 1984, he won the Eastman Award as the nation's top college player (photo at right).

The Second "Shot"

At the end of that season, the Tar Heels made it to the national championship game against the Georgetown Hoyas. There were 61,000 fans packed into the New Orleans Superdome.

Slow at first, the game sped up to an intense level. With 32 seconds left, the Tar Heels trailed by one point. They called time-out.

Coach Smith told the team to get the ball to Michael. "Make it, Michael," he then said. The game was once again in Michael's hands.

A teammate passed the ball to Michael. The Hoyas' defense rushed toward him. In the stands, Michael's father shut his eyes.

Michael stayed calm. He took the shot. The crowd screamed. Swish! UNC had taken the lead, 63-62. Within seconds, the buzzer went off. UNC had won the national championship. Michael had made "the shot" once more.

A National Star Is Born

After the championship game, Michael's father said, "Your life will never be the same after the shot." He was right.

On the UNC campus and around the country, Michael became a star. Photos of "the shot" appeared in newspapers and magazines across the country. But this fame had a downside.

Now, everywhere Michael went, people followed him. This sometimes bothered him. However, his desire to be the best helped him rise above the problem.

Throughout the summer after his freshman year, Michael trained hard. He worked on his shooting and his ball control. As the new college year started, Michael was one of the best players on the team. Michael pushed himself hard. He also began to push his teammates.

---

downside: an unfavorable side

The Cost of Winning

Not everyone liked being pushed hard by Michael. As he gained confidence, Michael pushed harder. Even at practices, he became very intense. His competitive nature did not always win him friends. Sometimes Michael felt very alone.

Michael's competitive spirit puzzled his college friends. Whatever they played, even card games, Michael had to win. If he lost, he got angry. His drive to win sometimes got him in trouble and cost him friends.

Michael continued to study hard and spend every spare minute training. Newspapers began to write about his talent. During the summer, Michael went on tour overseas with the Tar Heels. He found out that he enjoyed meeting other people and learning about different cultures.

By the time summer was over, Michael weighed 190 pounds (86 kilograms) and had grown to 6 feet 6 inches (2 meters) tall. He was ready for some new challenges.

The 1984 Olympics

One of Michael's dreams was to play for the U.S. Olympic basketball team. In 1984, that dream came true. He was selected to play in the Olympics held in Los Angeles.

Past U.S. teams had dominated Olympic basketball. Prior to the 1984 Olympics, U.S. teams had won 69 of 70 games.

When Michael and the 1984 U.S. team got to the Olympics, they did not spoil that winning record. The Americans defeated each team one by one. They beat all eight teams they played. They won the gold medal.

Michael had the highest scoring average on the U.S. Olympic team. The Spanish team's coach could not believe what he had seen. He said, "He's not human. He's a rubber man." At the Olympics, Michael proved that he had the talent to play at a higher level.

---

dominate: to take control of or rule

Michael averaged 17 points per game in the 1984 Olympics.

Life-changing Decision

To play his best, Michael had to feel challenged. Michael had become so good that he no longer saw college basketball as a challenge. He thought about leaving school to play in the National Basketball Association (NBA).

Both Michael's father and Coach Smith thought Michael was ready for the pros. Coach Smith was very unselfish to advise Michael to turn pro. Michael was one of the main reasons his UNC team had won a national championship in 1982.

On May 5, 1984, Michael and Coach Smith announce that Michael will turn pro.

But Michael still had doubts. He liked UNC. He didn't want to leave school without a degree. What if his basketball career didn't work out?

Michael's mother did not want him to leave college. She knew that, unlike a basketball career, education lasts forever. No one can take it away. A knee injury doesn't cancel your college degree. For the sake of his future, Michael's mother wanted him to get the best education possible.

Finally, Michael decided to turn pro. But he promised his mother that he would still finish his degree. He would use the next two summers, basketball's off-season, to complete his college courses. A press conference was called. Michael announced his decision. He was going pro.

degree: the rank given by a college or university to a student who has completed a course of study

*Michael shows his new
Chicago Bulls uniform.*

CHAPTER 3

Early Years in the NBA

Michael Jordan had decided to turn pro. How well would he play in the NBA? Would wanting to win be enough? Was he really good enough to play with the best? Michael needed to find out.

Bullish on Michael Jordan

At the NBA draft in 1984, the Chicago Bulls picked Michael. The Bulls had a losing record. Of course, this gave Michael a challenge. "Chicago is a young team, and we have a lot of hard work ahead. The only way for the Bulls to go is up, and I'm really looking forward to making a contribution," he said.

Everyone in Chicago had high hopes for Michael. Now Michael was under a new kind of pressure.

A Superstar in the Making

Michael found that the pro game was much harder than college basketball. The players were bigger, stronger, quicker, and better. These challenges made Michael work harder than ever. He began to improve his already good skills.

Early in his NBA career, Michael liked playing on the road more than at home. People expected teams to lose when they played away. This gave Michael a greater challenge and pushed him to play even harder.

Fans loved Michael's high-flying dunks. Crowds cheered him like a rock star. This spurred Michael on. He wanted to please the fans.

Soon companies were asking Michael to advertise their products. One company named a shoe "Air Jordan" after him. People started calling him Air Jordan, too. Michael was really beginning to fly.

Rough Road to Stardom

Stardom wasn't all good, though. Some teammates were jealous of Michael's skills and his fans. They accused him of stealing glory from them. They grumbled about playing "Michaelball."

Compete or Cooperate?

The players from other teams were also jealous. They said the Bulls were a one-man show. They fouled Michael all the time. This sparked his competitive spirit. It drove him to want revenge. He decided to be better than all the other NBA players, especially the ones who criticized him.

But revenge doesn't help basketball teams win championships. Slowly, Michael learned this lesson. Just as his parents told him to rise above racism, he rose above revenge. He began to pay more attention to his teammates during games. He realized what Coach Smith had always taught—it is important to be a team player.

revenge: a chance to get back at another
criticize: to find fault with

Injured!

One game in 1985, disaster struck. Michael fell and didn't get up. His teammates gathered around him. Michael was helped off the court.

The team trainer said Michael's ankle was sprained. Michael expected to miss just three games. Then a scan revealed a broken bone in Michael's foot. He was going to miss six weeks.

During his recovery, Michael sat on the sidelines. He hated being out of the action. He couldn't bear watching. He wanted to play. To cheer him up, someone challenged him to shoot from his seat. It didn't take long for Michael to start swishing baskets from his seat!

Michael is sidelined with a cast on his foot.

disaster: something that causes great harm
scan: an electronic image used to study the inside of the body

Michael went home to Wilmington, North Carolina to rest his ankle. He watched games on TV with Coach Smith. He worked on completing his college degree. He lifted weights. Time passed. The bone wouldn't heal.

Doctors told Michael he would be out even longer than expected. Michael was worried. His fans were worried. Although Michael couldn't play, fans still voted him onto the All-Star team!

Finally, the cast was taken off. The doctors told Michael to rest. But Michael felt he had sat long enough. Secretly, he began to practice. In April, he returned to the Bulls' starting lineup. He had missed 64 games. He amazed everyone with his determination to play again.

determination: the quality of setting one's mind to doing something

Grounding Air Jordan

Michael was becoming a superstar. Opponents had to figure out how to stop him. To ground Air Jordan, teams used a special play called "The Jordan Rules." The play was simple. Stop Michael at any cost. This usually meant sending him crashing to the floor before he reached the basket.

Of course, "The Jordan Rules" made Michael try even harder. It made him want to win even more. And he did.

Opponents tried to stop Michael at any cost.

Better Bulls

Michael often got angry when he was fouled. But Michael learned to direct his anger into his game rather than against his opponents. If someone pushed him down, he pushed himself to score even more points. He also played even better defense. He learned this was a much better way of dealing with anger.

Michael scored. He broke records. But he would not be content until the Bulls won an NBA championship ring. He couldn't do that on his own.

At the request of Coach Phil Jackson, Michael began to encourage his teammates more. He became a team leader, and the Bulls got better. In 1988, they made it to the NBA championship playoffs.

In the first round of the playoffs, the Bulls played the Cleveland Cavaliers. The Cavs had already beaten the Bulls six times that season. It was going to be a tough challenge.

---

playoff: a contest played to decide a championship

"The Shot"—Again!

By game five, the series against the Cavaliers was tied 2-2. The Bulls had lost game four. Michael felt he was to blame for the loss. He had missed a free throw late in the game. As Michael entered the Cavaliers' home court, the Cleveland fans booed. The missed shot and the booing fans motivated Michael.

In the second half, Michael began to raise the level of his game. The Bulls grabbed a slight lead late in the game. The Cavs' fans weren't booing anymore. They were quiet.

With just 13 seconds to go, the Cavs called a time-out to set up a play. The play worked as Craig Ehlo drove to the hoop to score. Now the Cavs led 100-99 with three seconds left. The home crowd smelled victory.

The Bulls now called time-out. Everyone, including the Cavs, knew what the play would be. The Bulls had to get the ball to Michael.

---

motivate: to drive to a goal

Play resumed. The roar of the Cavs' fans was deafening. Michael got the ball. He remembered what Coach Smith had always said. "This is fun," he reminded himself.

Two seconds remained. Michael dribbled toward the top of the key. One second. With Ehlo all over him, Michael went up for a jump shot. As Michael released the ball, the crowd went silent. The ball floated toward the hoop. The basket seemed to be pulling the ball toward it.

As the buzzer sounded to end the game, the ball went through the net. The final score was 101-100. The Bulls had won the game and the playoff. Michael soared into the air with joy. He was flying.

The Cavs were stunned. Their 20,000 fans went totally silent. How could anyone make that shot?

Everyone knew Michael was good. But at that moment, Michael Jordan became better than good. He became a superstar.

Michael displays superstar moves.

CHAPTER 4

The Glory Years

Michael Jordan was now a superstar. But how could he top "the shot"? What would be his next challenge? What if people expected him to be a superstar in every game? How could he keep up?

The "Three-Peat"

At this point in Michael Jordan's career, he had made "the shot" three times. Once in high school, once in college, and now in the NBA, Michael had drilled an incredible winning shot. Michael had raised his game to superstar status.

In 1991, Michael won his first NBA championship. But one wasn't enough. Michael set his eyes on another number three—three straight NBA titles. That's exactly what he and the Chicago Bulls accomplished, as they won two more titles, in 1992 and 1993.

"The Dream Team"

Michael had won Olympic gold in 1984 as a college player. In 1992, he had another chance to be an Olympian. The Olympic Games were being held in Barcelona, Spain. For the first time, professional basketball players could play in the games.

The players on Team U.S.A. were truly amazing. They quickly became known as "the Dream Team." They were the best of the best. Of course, Michael Jordan was among them. Now he was excited for the chance to play with the greatest, not just against them.

Michael said that the only team that could beat the Dream Team was—the Dream Team! He was right. Team U.S.A. stormed through the Olympics, winning every game. The gold medal was theirs.

---

professional: a person who is paid money to play a sport

Michael was Team U.S.A.'s top scorer. Even among his Dream Team teammates, he was the greatest. Michael Jordan had become the best of the best, the best in the world.

Michael and Clyde Drexler enjoy themselves at the Olympic medal ceremony.

The Dream Team

Michael Jordan

Larry Bird

Magic Johnson

Karl Malone

Charles Barkley

Patrick Ewing

David Robinson

Scottie Pippen

Chris Mullin

Clyde Drexler

Christian Laettner

Tragedy

Michael's best friend was his father, James Jordan. One evening in 1993, James was driving home from a funeral. The car he was in was a gift from Michael. James felt tired and pulled over. He dozed off by his open window.

James wore two rings that Michael had given him. One was Michael's 1986 All-Star Game ring. Another was a replica of his first NBA championship ring. As James slept, two young men approached him. They shot and killed him. They stole the rings and the car. Fortunately, both robbers were caught. They will be in prison for the rest of their lives.

The Jordan family was heartbroken. Michael tried his best to remain positive. He said, "Some children never have their fathers for any years, and I had mine for almost 31. No one can convince me that I was unlucky."

---

replica: an exact copy

A Break from Basketball

Soon after his father's death, Michael retired from basketball for the first time. He had become tired and was no longer challenged with the game. He also liked to think that his father saw his last game. Michael's NBA career scoring average was 32.3 points per game. It was the NBA's all-time best.

Michael felt he had nothing left to prove. Reporters asked what he was going to do. Michael's answer became famous. He replied that he was going to watch the grass grow and then go out and cut it.

But Michael needed a challenge. That's how Michael Jordan is. In 1994, he decided to take up baseball. He had been a star baseball player as a boy. But he had not played for years. Michael wanted to try to be a major league baseball player with the Chicago White Sox. This decision surprised everyone.

Minor League Michael

Before he could get to the major leagues, Michael had to play minor league baseball. Michael's minor league pay was nothing compared with his salary with the Bulls. But he was not playing for the money. He was playing to fulfill a boyhood dream.

Michael did miss the comfortable life of the NBA, though. He didn't like the no-frills traveling style of the minor league team. He couldn't stand the uncomfortable road trips and the cheap hotel rooms. So he bought the team a luxury bus for traveling.

Michael fulfilled his boyhood dream to play professional baseball.

no-frills: lacking in costly or comfortable things

"I've Failed . . .
and That Is Why I Succeed."

Michael trained hard to become a baseball player. Although he was not great, he was not awful. He showed promise.

Then a baseball strike stopped the games. At that point, Michael decided he was not good enough to play professional baseball without a lot more effort. He gave up his baseball dream. Some people criticized him. But he had tried. He had challenged himself once again.

Whether he was playing basketball or baseball, Michael kept a positive attitude. One of Michael's ads shows this attitude. The ad tells how many times he has missed shots, and how many times he has lost games. In the ad, Michael says that he succeeds because he has failed.

Michael failed at baseball, but he built on his failure. He picked himself up. And then he surprised the world. Michael went back to the Bulls again.

"I'm Back!"

In 1995, Michael returned to basketball. He told the world his plans in two words: "I'm back." Michael knew he would not be the same player he had been. He knew he would have to change his game to be a winner again.

Adjusting His Game

At first, Michael was very rusty on the court. He didn't stay rusty for long, however. He also showed he could do much more than score, as he proved during one game with the New York Knicks.

With just over three seconds left, the score was tied. Michael got the ball as usual. The defense went after him. This left teammate Bill Wennington wide open. He passed to Wennington, who put the ball right in the net. The Bulls had won.

Michael no longer needed to make "the shot" himself to help the Bulls win. Age and experience had added wisdom to his fierce spirit.

Michael "Air Jordan" had always wanted to win. But over the years he had learned that wanting to win wasn't enough. He had learned that winning took failure, determination, and teamwork. With those ingredients, both he and his teammates could become the winners they wanted to be.

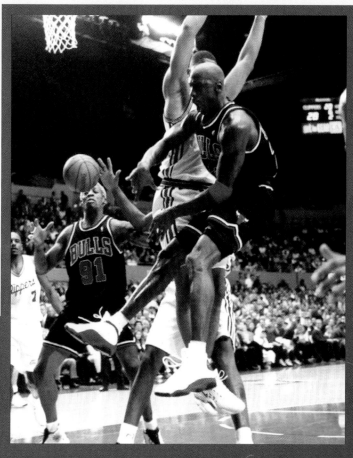

Michael learned to involve his teammates more in the game.

Michael's intense desire to play drove him to try for another "three-peat."

CHAPTER 5

Moving On

Michael and the Chicago Bulls won their fourth NBA title in 1996. Still, many critics thought Michael's return to basketball was a mistake. He had left the game on top, a three-time NBA champion. Now he had nowhere to go but down. Why come back?

Not Ready to Quit

In 1995-96, the first year Michael came back, the Bulls won their fourth NBA championship. Now Michael found another challenge. He wanted to lead the Bulls to another "three-peat." But it wouldn't be easy. When they made the NBA championship finals in 1997, he found out just how hard it could be.

Pushing Too Hard

It was the fifth game in the 1997 NBA championship finals. The Bulls fans were waving banners, chanting, going crazy.

The Bulls were playing the Utah Jazz. If anyone was going to beat the Bulls, it was the Jazz. The Jazz had some superstars of their own. These included veterans Karl Malone and John Stockton. After four games, the series was even at 2-2.

That day of game five, Michael awoke at 3:30 a.m. He was sick and getting worse. He felt weak. He had a fever. The coaches listed him as "uncertain" to play.

Challenges always drove Michael. This time, however, his body was stopping him. Scottie Pippen, a teammate, saw Michael arrive for the game. He didn't think Michael would even be able to get his uniform on, let alone play. But Michael did.

---

veteran: a person who has had long experience in a job

Playing Really Sick

The game started. Michael thought he would pass out. Sweat poured from his body. He played poorly. Somehow, though, he grew stronger in the second quarter. But it wasn't enough. The Jazz led 53-49 at halftime. The announcers were sure the Jazz would win.

During halftime, Michael drank juice and ate some applesauce. He needed energy. When the second half began, Michael's head was spinning. But he believed that if he gave up, so would his team.

So Michael gave everything. Late in the game, so weak at times he could barely walk, he sank a three-pointer. The Bulls inched ahead. As the final buzzer sounded, the score was 90-88. Michael had done it. He had led the Bulls one step closer to their fifth NBA championship.

Not Worth the Risk

Michael had to be helped off the court. He was completely drained. His need to win had made him give everything. Sports fans thought Michael was the bravest.

But Michael had risked more important things to win this time. He had risked his health. A healthy Michael was far more important to the family he loved than any game. Michael's love of winning sometimes went too far. He later admitted that it was a mistake to play in that game.

Michael continued to fly in the 1997-98 season. In 1998, the Bulls won their second "three-peat," defeating the Utah Jazz in game six. Michael had achieved another of his goals. In the final game, he even made "the shot" one more time to win the championship.

Michael Jordan holds the
1998 NBA championship trophy.

The First "Three-Peat"

1 9 9 1 The Bulls beat the Los Angeles Lakers 108-101 in game five to win the NBA championship.

1 9 9 2 The Bulls beat the Portland Trail Blazers 97-93 in game six to win their second straight NBA title.

1 9 9 3 The Bulls beat the Phoenix Suns 99-98 in game six. They are the first team to win three straight NBA championships since 1966.

The Second "Three-Peat"

1996 Jordan returns to the Bulls, who beat the Seattle Supersonics to win their fourth NBA championship.

1997 In game five, a very ill Jordan helps the Bulls come from 16 points down to beat the Utah Jazz. The Bulls capture their fifth title in the next game.

1998 The Bulls defeat the Utah Jazz for their second "three-peat" and sixth NBA championship. Jordan scores the winning points in the final game.

Game Over

The 1998-99 season was late starting. There was a "lockout." Players and team owners were fighting over salaries. Coach Phil Jackson announced that he was leaving the Bulls. Michael didn't want to play for another coach. Plus, Michael had achieved as much as he felt he could. He had flown higher than any NBA player in history.

The lockout ended on January 6, 1999. One week later, Michael Jordan retired from the NBA for the second time.

Keeping Busy

After he retired, Michael stayed plenty busy. Family matters most to Michael. He is married and has three children, Jeffrey, James, and Jasmine. He also has many business interests. He supports charities. He gives his time and money to good causes. He acts in movies and TV commercials. On Jan. 19, 2000, Michael became part owner of the Washington Wizards, another NBA team.

---

lockout: when a company refuses to let workers come to work

*Michael and his wife Juanita
discuss his retirement from
the NBA.*

"The Game I Love"

Michael likes to work with other basketball players. And of course, he loves to play basketball. In fact, he enjoys both so much, he decided to return to the NBA as a player.

"I am returning as a player to the game I love," Michael announced on Sept. 25, 2001. Michael signed a two-year contract to play with the Washington Wizards. "I feel there is no better way of teaching young players than to be on the court with them as a fellow player," he said.

Michael said he would donate his salary for the season. He would give it to help those who suffered most from the terrorist attacks in the United States on Sept. 11, 2001.

After his first preseason game, someone asked Michael what lessons his younger teammates might learn from watching him play. "Don't think that you know everything," he said, "because this game will teach you something new every day. It's still teaching me."

Michael drives to the basket as a Washington Wizard.

Epilogue

1983	Sporting News' Player of the Year
1984	Sporting News' Player of the Year
1984	Wooden Award Winner
1984	Naismith Award Winner
1985	NBA Rookie of the Year
1985	All-Rookie First Team
1985	All-NBA Second Team
1987	Slam-Dunk Champion
1987	All-NBA First Team
1987	Scoring Champion
1988	All-Star Game MVP
1988	Slam-Dunk Champion
1988	NBA MVP
1988	All-NBA First Team
1988	All-Defensive First Team
1988	Scoring Champion
1988	Defensive Player of the Year
1988	Steals Champion
1989	All-NBA First Team
1989	All-Defensive First Team
1989	Sporting News' Player of the Year
1989	Scoring Champion
1990	All-NBA First Team
1990	All-Defensive First Team
1990	Scoring Champion
1990	Steals Champion
1991	All-NBA First Team
1991	All-Defensive First Team
1991	NBA MVP

NBA Finals MVP	1991
Scoring Champion	1991
All-NBA First Team	1992
All-Defensive First Team	1992
NBA MVP	1992
NBA Finals MVP	1992
Scoring Champion	1992
All-NBA First Team	1993
All-Defensive First Team	1993
NBA Finals MVP	1993
Scoring Champion	1993
Steals Champion	1993
All-Star Game MVP	1996
Scoring Champion	1996
NBA MVP	1996
NBA Finals MVP	1996
All-NBA First Team	1996
All-Defensive First Team	1996
All-Star Game MVP	1996
Scoring Champion	1997
NBA Finals MVP	1997
All-NBA First Team	1997
All-Defensive First Team	1997
All-Star Game MVP	1998
NBA MVP	1998
NBA Finals MVP	1998
Scoring Champion	1998
All-NBA First Team	1998
All-Defensive First Team	1998
Member of the "NBA at 50" team	1998

Glossary

competitive: badly wanting to win; always seeking to do better than others

criticize: to find fault with

defender: a player who tries to keep the other team from scoring

degree: the rank given by a college or university to a student who has completed a course of study

desperately: with a willingness to do anything

determination: the quality of setting one's mind to doing something

disaster: something that causes great harm

discipline: control over the way a person behaves

dominate: to take control of or rule

downside: an unfavorable side

intensity: strong feelings

lockout: when a company refuses to let workers come to work

motivate: to drive to a goal

no-frills: lacking in costly or comfortable things

playoff: a contest played to decide a championship

professional: a person who is paid money to play a sport

replica: an exact copy

revenge: a chance to get back at another

scan: an electronic image used to study the inside of the body

sharecropper: a person who farms land owned by another person

varsity: the main team that represents a school

veteran: a person who has had long experience in a job

Bibliography

Aaseng, Nathan. *Sports Great Michael Jordan.* Rev. ed. Springfield, N.J.: Enslow, 1997.

Christopher, Matt. *On the Court with. . . Michael Jordan.* Boston: Little, Brown and Company, 1996.

Jordan, Michael. *For the Love of the Game: My Story.* Edited by Mark Vancil. New York: Crown Publishers, 1998.

Lazenby, Roland. *Chicago Bulls: The Authorized Pictorial.* Arlington, Texas: Summit Publishing Group, 1997.

Lipsyte, Robert. *Michael Jordan: A Life Above the Rim.* New York: HarperCollins Publishers, 1994.

Lovitt, Chip. *Michael Jordan.* Scholastic Biography. New York: Scholastic, 1999.

Mullin, Chris. *Basketball.* DK Superguides. New York: Dorling Kindersley, 2000.

Useful Addresses

Chicago Bulls Fan Club
1901 West Madison Street
Chicago, IL 60612-2459

Naismith Memorial Basketball Hall of Fame
1150 West Columbus Avenue
Springfield, MA 01105

Internet Sites

Michael Jordan: Shooting His Way to Greatness
http://www.usatoday.com/sports/basketba/skn/
    jordan.htm

Michael Jordan: Sportsline.com
http://jordan.sportsline.com/

Naismith Memorial Basketball Hall of Fame
http://www.hoophall.com/

NBA.com
http://www.nba.com/

Index